Evaluate to Enrich

by Harold J. Westing

"I don't think I should be evaluated, after all I'm not a professional teacher." "Evaluation isn't necessary for church teachers; after all, doesn't the Lord bless all our labors for him?" "I only agreed to teach because no one else would; so I don't think anyone should criticize what I do." Have you ever expressed comments like these? They are commonly voiced by some members of church teaching staffs when the subject of evaluation is mentioned. For some, evaluation has become equated with criticism.

This attitude is unfortunate because evaluation (and, in a sense, criticism) can be a useful tool for improving the quality of teaching, when it is carried out in a constructive and loving manner. Evaluation should more appropriately be equated with helping teachers reach their full potential.

Once a teaching staff fully understands its real value, evaluation can result in substantial growth of a church's educational program.

Why Evaluation Is Important

There are at least three reasons why you as a Christian teacher should want to be evaluated and to evaluate your own teaching: (1) The Bible suggests the need for continual evaluation. (2) Informal evaluation continually takes place. (3) Evaluation promotes effectiveness.

The Bible suggests the need for continual evaluation—The limited space of this article allows the mention of only the key Scripture passages that refer to the need for evaluation.

God himself made the first evaluation after creating the world when the Bible says, "God saw every thing that he had made, and, behold it was very good" (Gen. 1:31).

I Corinthians 11 suggests that Christians ought to evaluate themselves before coming to the Lord's table. This same principle can be applied to teachers who come week after week to teach without first examining themselves to see if they are doing the best possible job.

The writer of Proverbs tersely sums up the need for teachers to take an honest look at their ministries. "Like an earring of gold or an ornament of fine gold is a wise man's rebuke to a listening ear. By wisdom a house is built, and through knowledge its rooms are filled with rare and beautiful treasures. Whoever loves discipline loves knowledge, but he who hates correction is stupid" (Prov. 25:12; 24:3, 4; 12:1; NIV).

Hebrews 10:24 encourages all Christians to consider how they may spur one another on toward love and good deeds. This is what should be occuring in the New Testament church—and especially among its teachers and leaders.

> **Effectiveness depends on pinpointing those techniques and procedures needing improvement. The best way to do this is continual evaluation.**

Informal Evaluation continually takes place—Each time a student brings a friend to your class or enthusiastically participates in classroom activities you are receiving a positive evaluation. On the other hand, a negative evaluation is evidenced when students drop out or refuse to cooperate. Every week during every class you are being informally evaluated. If for no other reason, you ought to evaluate yourself lest in the informal evaluation which your students conduct, continual negative grades cause them to drop out.

Evaluation promotes effectiveness—The goals of your teaching ministry in the church are three-fold: evangelizing—encouraging students to receive Christ as Savior; edifying—bringing students to maturity in Christ; and equipping—preparing students to serve Christ.

You as a mature Christian teacher always should be seeking to accomplish these goals and should not be satisfied until you are doing it in the most effective way. Effectiveness depends on pinpointing those techniques and procedures needing improvement. The best way to do this is continual evaluation.

When you catch this vision and approach your ministry with a sense of mission for God, effectiveness is the result.

Getting Started With Evaluation

To get started evaluating your teaching, there are several steps that need to be followed.

Establish a standard—In order to evaluate, a standard needs to be established. If your church has not formulated such a standard, this is where you need to begin. Perhaps your board of Christian education will do this for you or maybe a group of the current teachers could get together to formulate it, or, if you are evaluating yourself, establish your own.

To formulate a standard, decide what qualifications the ideal teacher should possess. To accomplish this, answer the following questions.

1. How much time should a teacher spend in Bible study and prayer each day or week?
2. How much time should a teacher spend in preparation each week?
3. What books and materials should a teacher use while studying a lesson?
4. What types of teaching methods should a teacher employ?
5. What materials and equipment should a teacher use while teaching a class?
6. How can a teacher structure an effective learning environment?
7. How many minutes before class should a teacher arrive?
8. What attitude should a teacher have toward opinions that might differ from his own?
9. How should a teacher maintain contact with the faithful attenders outside of class?
10. How should a teacher contact students who have been absent?
11. Under what circumstances should a teacher urge students to accept Christ as Savior?
12. What church services should a teacher attend each week?
13. What Sunday school related meetings should a teacher attend?
14. What responsibilities does a teacher have to other staff members?
15. What opportunities should a teacher take advantage of to cultivate teaching skills?

Once these standards have been established you might suggest that they be incorporated into a job description and distributed to all future teachers.

Most governments have a department or bureau of standards and measurements. This department establishes an official standard by which all commodities can be compared and evaluated. A department of standards is important to the well-being of a nation. An evaluation standard serves in the same capacity. It gives teachers a norm by which they can examine themselves.

Evaluate in the light of that standard—Any evaluation instrument ought to reflect your church's educational philosophy. Evaluation can be done by someone observing you in action or by applying the standards on your own. The important thing is, once the standard has been established, there must be a meaningful and honest way to evaluate the degrees to which these objectives are being accomplished.

> **The goal of evaluation in your teaching ministry is not to condemn you but to help you improve as a teacher.**

An evaluation should not be a judging experience. Judging has the sense of condemning. Evaluation has to do with enriching or improving your ministry. Someone has wisely called evaluations 'helpacisms,' rather than criticisms. The goal of evaluation in your teaching ministry is not to condemn you but to help you improve as a teacher.

No evaluation will be of any benefit unless you come to the place where you can evaluate yourself and you have a strong desire to improve your ministry. That doesn't mean that you can't have others help you. In fact, it will almost be essential for you to have someone aid you in the process.

Self-evaluation is difficult because of the following two factors. First, you can't

Vol. 1, Session 7

T here can be no greater frustration than failing to communicate! One person contends, "But I said. . .," while the other replies, "But I thought you meant. . ." Failure to communicate is a common problem everywhere. It is compounded by cultural and language barriers.

Communication and Teaching

C ommunication is the process of conveying a thought or concept from one person to another. In teaching, this process is vital. Teaching is communicating. Thus the thoughts or concepts conveyed by the teacher must be grasped by the student if learning is to take place.

Student interest is of utmost importance. Communication breaks down if the student is bored or distracted, or if the teacher is endeavoring to communicate on a level either above or below that of the students. In Christian teaching, the concern goes beyond the learning of facts to an application of these facts which results in changing the heart and mind of the student. Since you as a Christian teacher teach life-changing truths, you must not bore your students.

How can classes be kept exciting? How can you teach the Word so students' lives are changed? One method is to use every available channel of communication. These are sight,

Audiovisuals: Tools For Teaching

Dennis Bouchard

sound, taste, touch, and smell—the five senses. Through these senses, the brain receives information.

You need to involve as much of the student's attention and personality as possible. By utilizing more than one channel of communication, the student is drawn into the class session and will remember more of the presentation than he otherwise would. The greater the number of channels used, the greater the level of learning involvement. When verbal communication is supplemented with a visual aid or a learning activity, your students will be attentive. Attentive students will respond with immediate feedback or with

inner reflection. This also causes them to think about possible applications. Application to life is a significant goal of Bible teaching.

A wide range of audiovisual possibilities are available to you. Explore these with a desire to discover what kinds are suitable to the age level you teach and how to use them effectively. Bible truths are exciting. Teach the Word so that students want to learn it, apply it, and grow in the knowledge of the Lord.

Audiovisuals and the Bible

Scripture demonstrates God's use of visual aids. God created man in his image, including the ability to communicate. Designed with the five senses, man is able to receive and give information in a variety of ways. And God makes use of his design.

Genesis records God's command for Noah to build an ark as a direct warning to the people of a coming catastrophe. The rainbow arched in the sky reminds us of God's promise to never again destroy the earth with a flood. Jesus, the master teacher, is a model to follow. Frequently making reference to everyday objects, he illustrated God's principles. Bread, a staple food in the Middle East, became a symbol of the "bread of life" needed for spiritual growth. Sheep and shepherds dotted the hillsides; Jesus illustrated his love and concern for the people by the relationship between the shepherd and his sheep. Jesus washed the disciples' feet to clarify their roles as servants. Abiding in Christ was made clear in the picture of the branches abiding in the vine. Christ coming to earth, his miracles, crucifixion, and resurrection—all exemplify God's use of visuals to teach about himself.

God uses more than one channel of communication to teach his children. Follow his example and wisely use the available ways to teach God's Word.

Tools For Teaching

There is a wide variety of audiovisual tools and many ways to use each one. Since churches vary in their equipment, each teacher should discover what materials his church offers.

The following sections contain a brief description of, as well as suggestions for, effective use of several audiovisual teaching tools. They are grouped in general categories to provide for quick reference.

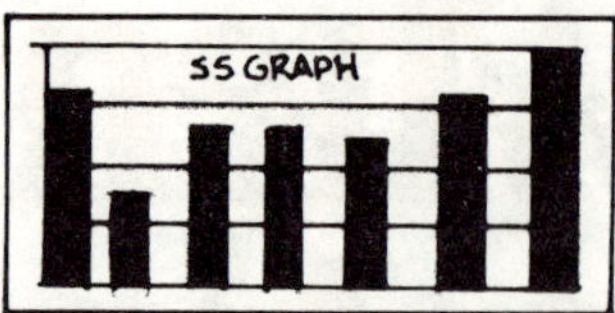

Non-projected Visuals

Bulletin boards are "silent teachers." By using good visual form, attractive colors, and effective pictures, a bulletin board can emphasize, remind, review, introduce, or announce a variety of subjects. Keep it current for maximum impact on the viewer.

Chalkboards are available in many classrooms. If you write as you speak, you must be careful to speak to the class, *not* to the chalkboard.

Charts can be used to show progression. A time line is an example. The life of Abraham or Paul will be remembered better if the class is involved in drawing the chart. This chart can be placed on display in the classroom. Rolls of shelf or freezer paper can be used for a long, continuous chart.

Graphs present statistical or financial information such as Sunday school growth or financial trends in the church. These statistics can be presented in the form of a pie or circle graph, a vertical bar graph, or a horizontal line graph.

Flannelgraphs are effective teaching tools. Adhesive-backed, flocked strips can be attached to mounted pictures or strips of posterboard. Draw pictures or print words, symbols, or statements on the face of the posterboard. These visuals will adhere to the flannelgraph and can be positioned or removed as the lesson is presented. Practice is necessary for effective use of this tool—even when utilizing professionally-produced flannelgraph stories.

Globes and maps provide a geographic perspective. Bible history comes alive when the students see the migration, residence, and obstacles of historical people. Emphasizing missions is aided by showing the location of countries where the Lord's work is being carried on.

Learning centers are displays of materials assembled for the purpose of student viewing or for providing a learning activity. A table with a selection of books or an exhibit of items relating to a study such as the Holy Land, focuses attention and provides another source of new information.

Models, being representative of something larger, help convey details and surroundings of Bible events. Exhibits of Solomon's temple, the tabernacle, or a house or village in Bible times help transport students back to the scenes of their Bible study. Preparing a model is also an excellent means of involving students in a meaningful learning activity.

Objects from everyday life can be used to teach principles of the Christian life and illustrate Bible concepts. Some potted plants grown in different soils might illustrate the parable of the sower. Other familiar items can illustrate some aspect of God's truth.

Pictures are the most common visual teaching resources. Whether prepared commercially, gathered from magazines, or drawn by hand, they can be adapted to a multitude of uses. Pictures can be used to illustrate a Bible story, enhance a bulletin board, draw attention to a poster, or provide a pattern for a handwork project. Their versatility of use is only outweighted by the multitude of pictures available.

Pictures can be organized and filed by general subject headings for future use.

Posters capture attention and quickly convey a single thought. They can be used in Bible memorization and in teaching biblical principles. Class members can design and

Dramatizing the Lesson

Dr. and Mrs. Ted Faszer

Biblical Precedents for Using Dramatization

Teaching is more than telling. In the Bible we see that when God wanted to make an impression on people he often used action along with words, and sometimes used dramatic action alone to communicate his message. God made us and knows how we learn best. He knows that actions often make a more profound impact upon us than words alone. As teachers today we may learn from God and from the Bible that drama is an effective tool for influencing our students' knowledge, attitudes, and skills. Drama captures attention, imparts knowledge, appeals to our emotions, challenges our reason and will, and provides opportunities for us to act out our convictions.

God Used Drama

Think of the many ways God used dramatic actions and events to communicate with people. When God called Moses, he captured Moses' attention through the unusual and dramatic action of a burning bush (Exod. 3). When God wanted Pharoah to let His people go, God used both words and actions. But Pharoah understood God's power best through His dramatic actions in the plagues (Exod. 5—12). God commanded his people to observe feasts which dramatized the mighty acts of God and the responsibilities of the people toward God, their creator and sustainer. The drama and symbolism of these feasts helped parents explain God's saving plan to their children (Exod. 13). God commanded outward signs and symbols to be used to demonstrate the relationship of his people to himself: circumcision (Gen. 17); and frontlets (Exod. 13, Deut. 6, 11). Imagine the drama, pageantry, and color when Solomon and the people dedicated the Jerusalem temple for the worship of God (I Kings 8). God reminded his people that he was the one true God, and that Baal was a mere idol, not only by using the words of the prophet Elijah, but by dramatically sending fire and rain from heaven (I Kings 18). To the discouraged prophet, Elijah, he demonstrated his power through the earthquake, wind, and finally spoke through the still, small voice (I Kings 19). When God wanted to communicate with the arrogant and drunken Belshazzar, he dramatically used his hand to write on the wall of the king's palace (Dan. 5). When God wanted to convert a zealous persecutor of his church, he used a dramatic blinding light from heaven along with a voice to speak to Saul (Acts 9). A dramatic, convincing vision showed Peter God's plan to provide salvation for all races and nationalities (Acts 10).

Jesus Used Drama

Although God used words to tell people about himself for many centuries, we know God best through his action of becoming a man in Jesus Christ. That dramatic incarnation communicated ultimately and decisively the true nature of God. Jesus, through his actions and words, showed us who God is, and demonstrated God's redemptive plan for mankind.

While Jesus was on earth he demonstrated his mastery of teaching. Jesus used dramatizations frequently, and demonstrated a wide variety of dramatic forms. Jesus powerfully dramatized his conviction that the temple should be a house of prayer by expelling the corrupt money-changers (John 2). By bringing a small child into the midst of the crowd gathered about him, Jesus dramatized his teaching about the need for child-like faith (Matt. 18). Jesus made use of a dramatic silence and wrote in the dust with his finger, while the scribes and Pharisees contemplated their sins and realized they could not condemn the adulterous woman (John 8). Imagine the dramatic impact of Jesus' triumphal entry into Jerusalem. The crowds carpeted the road with their garments, waved palm branches, and sang hosanna, while Jesus rode the donkey, the animal which symbolized peace (Matt. 21). Baptism and the Lord's supper dramatically illustrate the relationship of the believer to Christ (Matt. 3, 26). And all of Jesus' miracles dramatically demonstrated his divine power.

Why should you use drama in your Christian education ministry? Because God and Jesus have shown that dramatic action is powerful in communicating spiritual truth. You can follow their example and become a more effective communicator of God's truth by using drama. Dramatizing your lessons can help make the truths of God's Word alive, meaningful, and life-changing for your students.

How and When to Use Drama

How can you decide when to use drama? Make sure that you have a worthwhile purpose for using it, whatever form you choose. Ask yourself questions about the drama: 1) Will this drama stimulate interest, arouse curiosity, or acquaint learners with a problem? 2) Does this drama provide a means by which to stimulate problem solving? 3) Is your plan for the drama specific enough to allow students to understand the purpose and structure of the activity? 4) Does your dramatization allow the student to plan and participate in the drama? 5) Is your dramatization flexible enough to take into account the ability and skill of each student so that the student can experience success and growth? 6) Does this drama enable students to express their thoughts or share with others? 7) Does this drama provide opportunity for students to apply Bible truth to their everyday experience? 8) Will this drama appeal to the students' emotions or deepen their appreciations?

Students' ideas can often make the dramatization more effective than if only the plans and ideas of the teacher are used. When teacher and students work together on a drama, the teacher can become more than a guide—he can learn along with the students.

The Role of the Leader

In order to dramatize a biblical truth, the teacher and students must first understand that truth. They must study the Scripture which may lead to the dramatic application of the Scripture.

Any teacher, given some basic instruction and a little practice, will be able to spot the dramatic possibilities in biblical incidents. Almost all of Jesus' parables lend themselves to dramatizations such as simple role plays, pantomimes, or puppet shows with sock or paper-bag puppets. The teacher can improve his story-telling abilities by memorizing the story and telling it with feeling. Perhaps someone in the congregation is gifted in writing and would help the teacher in writing more complex dramas. Every age group is able to use drama if the teacher is careful to choose dramatic forms appropriate to the age, abilities, and interests of the class.

The teacher, as the key to the success of drama, must be willing to become personally involved in the dramatization, but should be careful to take the lead only as long as the class needs direction. Then the teacher may step back, and let the students proceed with the dramatization. If a teacher of youth or adults is thoroughly prepared, confident, and unembarassed by the use of drama, and if the class understands what is expected of them, they will be more likely to participate freely. The teacher should never force or coerce the learner to participate in drama, but rather positively encourage each student to become involved and allow students the freedom not to participate if they desire.

Drama with Children

Dramatization involves the kinesthetic, or movement and feeling, sense which is important in the learning process of children. Children need many hands-on experiences in order to learn effectively. When beginning to use drama with young children, start with the non-verbal. Remember that at the start it is difficult for children to move and speak at

Training When Meeting

Vol. 1, Session 5

Teaching With Questions

Hugh M. Salisbury

What Is A Question?

Your mind is probably working right now to answer this query. And if so, you have a good clue to the answer. Almost automatically, your mind began searching for an answer—all because of four short words and a question mark.

A question, then, is a sentence which demands an answer. Educators since Socrates have found the question to be one of the most powerful teaching techniques.

Why are questions so powerful? Because they act as switches to "turn on" otherwise passive minds. A good question demands an answer because it introduces inbalance within the hearer. A question is like the first half of a suspense story. Once involved in the story, we are unsatisfied until we learn "whodunit." A question without an answer is like a hymn without an ending. It is like the first note of an "Amen" without the satisfying resolution of the final chord.

Jesus Used Questions

The Gospels record more than one hundred questions asked by Jesus. Surely this is proof of their potency. Christ did not ask in order to gain information for himself, but to lead his listeners into a personal search for the truth regarding themselves and his Father. At least three characteristics are basic to the questions used by Christ.

They Were Original

Jesus wove his questions out of the very yarn of his experience of Jewish life. When asked to show his credentials of authority, Christ answered with another question: "John's baptism—was it from heaven, or was it merely human?" Immediate communication resulted, for John the Baptist was very much upon the public tongue at the moment.

They Were Practical

When challenged about doing work on the Sabbath, Christ's response was geared to life-situations. "Which of you," he asked, "would not pull out a sheep which fell into a pit on the Sabbath day?" This practical question was followed by another: "Of how much more value is a man than a sheep?"

They Were Personal

Christ's questions worked their way into the hearts of individuals. "But whom shall *ye* say that I am?" And to Peter: "Lovest *thou me*?"

You Should Use Questions

Reflected in the three basics of Christ's questions are ingredients of every teaching situation. Three factors characterized the relationship between Christ and his disciples—and the same characteristics should be found in your questioning technique.

Directed to Students' Needs

Christ's questions were personal because he wanted to effect a change within his students, the disciples. Students' personal needs should be incorporated into your questions. As teacher, you should know the backgrounds of your students—their limitations, their level of understanding, their vocabulary, their interests. Frame your questions in light of this knowledge.

Focused on Practical Truths

Christ had certain truths to communicate to his dis-ciples—truths that affected them in practical, everyday living. You, too, have a body of material to communicate to your students. Good questions will tend to focus attention upon central issues in the classroom subject matter. If studying John the Baptist's ministry, don't ask: "What would you think of someone wearing camel's hair?" Such a question is open-ended and leads nowhere. Rather ask, "How did John's clothing fit in with his message?"

Reflect Your Own Originality

Christ did not attempt to communicate by using worn-out cliches. His presentation was original with himself, the Teacher. In your class, you are the personality who brings to life impersonal subject matter. It is up to you to frame questions that relate to the experiences and environment shared by yourself and your students. Let your questions fit naturally into your conversation, your tone of voice, your manner of speaking.

Good Questions Bring Results

The effectiveness of good questioning can be measured by considering how they will benefit the students, your material, and you as a teacher. Consider what good questions will do for each of these three areas.

For Your Students

A question will cause students to think. Some psychologists look upon the human brain as a sophisticated computer. Give it a problem and it sets about solving that problem on its own. If a student hears your question, he must either put it out of his mind or try to find the answer.

A question helps students to build upon past experiences. Properly and practically expressed, a question will tie

together old experiences into meaningful new patterns.

A question encourages students to express their thoughts in their own words. Verbal expression tends to "jell" vaguely formed ideas.

A question can result in a complete change of attitude within your students. Tell them to change, and they'll resist. Help them discover for themselves the reason for change, and their motivation will come from within. All of us tend to value our own discoveries above those of others.

For Your Subject Material

A good question will introduce something of a mystery into the materials. This arouses curiosity and stimulates interest in what otherwise might seem dry material.

A good question will help students to understand the facts. At times facts are not understood simply because they are not placed in proper relationship to one another. Christ's question about the Sabbath-breaking sheep in a pit, and his final query, "Of how much more value is a man than a sheep?" is a good example of new positioning of old facts.

A good question brings a wealth of previous experience and knowledge to bear upon the material at hand. Once the human "computer" is handed a problem it hunts through its

Vol. 1, Session 4

Student-Centered Teaching

Paul J. Loth

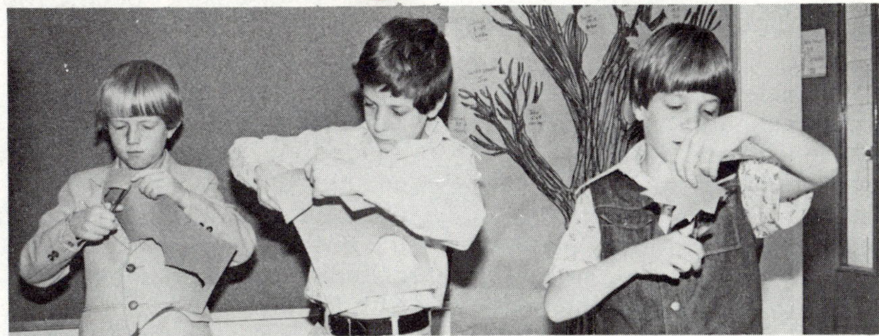

In the early twentieth century, novices learned professions through apprenticeship training. The trainee observed the master craftsman, received necessary instruction of the technique involved, and then practiced what he learned. Whether apprenticeship training or Christian education, involvement in learning is a major characteristic of effective teaching.

For years teachers have discussed approaches to the teaching-learning process. These approaches could be categorized as either "teacher-centered" or "student-centered." Those following teacher-centered methods present the truths of the lesson themselves. Most common among teacher-centered techniques are lecture and discussion. Teachers employing student-centered techniques provide learning opportunities and activities for the students. Techniques used in the student-centered approach are many and varied.

In either approach to the teaching-learning process, student involvement is essential. In the teacher-centered approach, such as lecture or discussion, students must be mentally involved in order for learning to take place. In the student-centered approach, such as group discussions or activities, students are directly involved in varied activities.

Reasons for Student-centered Teaching

Student-centered teaching is an attempt to bring about the involvement of each class member in learning Bible truths. This accomplishes several purposes:

Increased Learning

Learning takes place in a variety of ways, such as mental involvement in a teacher's presentation, direct study and research, discussion, or a specific learning activity. In each case, the student must be involved in order for learning to occur. A successful teacher will plan class sessions so that students can be directly involved in learning.

Jesus is the prime example. In Luke 9 and 10, the Lord sought to teach the disciples about ministry. He instructed them concerning what to do and then gave them opportunity to experience it. Upon their return, they shared what they had learned. Jesus taught them through their personal involvement.

Increased Enjoyment

Classes are both more beneficial and more enjoyable when students have an active role in various activities. In classes in which students participate, they are able to learn by working together.

Increased Fellowship

A major local church and Christian education objective is fellowship among believers (Acts 2:46, 47). Class fellowship becomes a reality when students are involved. They are then able to interact, share with each other, and become better acquainted as they are involved in learning Bible truths.

Increased Understanding of the Students

Student involvement also

allows the teacher to become better acquainted with the students' needs, capabilities, interests, and backgrounds. Teachers can learn how students interact by being observant during various activity periods, small group discussions, and general class discussion. Each teacher should try to talk with the students while projects are worked on and presented. This results in better understanding and reinforcement of learning.

Increased Student Abilities

Leadership and communication skills are evidenced and developed as students participate in class sessions. In youth and adult classes, student involvement is an important means of teacher training. Because of this, teachers should be alert to the expression of these abilities and provide positive encouragement to the students. Teachers can help the Christian education leadership by recommending class members evidencing certain abilities for various tasks.

Ways to Involve Students

Teachers sometimes experience difficulty knowing how to involve their students in the class session. *General discussion* is often used; but even a good class discussion usually only involves a minority of the students. Group and individual learning activities need to be incorporated into the lesson in order to involve all the students and provide a meaningful and enjoyable learning experience.

There are numerous possibilities for involving students in the lesson. The following list includes a few. Adapt them to fit your particular class situation and add to the list from your experience and ideas.

Small Groups

While individual class members are often lost in class discussions, small groups make it possible for each student to become directly involved in the lesson. It is best to limit the size of the groups to under five in order for individual interaction to occur. There are many possibilities for the use of small groups in teaching. Following are a few:

"Buzz" groups—Each group is asked to discuss a specific topic or Scripture and report back to the entire class at the end of a specified time limit.

Listening teams—The class is divided into several groups and each group is assigned a different question to answer on the basis of what is presented. Listening teams may be used with lecture, reading of a Bible passage, cassette tape, filmstrip, and film.

Interview—Students interview the person sitting next to them using questions provided. Often students interview several different people to receive more than one answer to each question. This is especially useful in the beginning of the lesson.

Occasionally a special guest who is knowledgeable in a particular subject will be interviewed by the class.

Neighbor nudging—Each class member is asked to share with his "neighbor" concerning a topic or question. This is a fast and easy means of getting students involved. It does not threaten students who have not been involved before.

Rotating discussion leaders— This technique involves several small groups and an equal number of discussion leaders. Each discussion leader has a different question or topic and shares with one group. At the end of a set time period, each leader moves to the next group. This process continues until all the leaders have shared with all the groups. The class session is often concluded with each

discussion leader participating in a panel in which the results of the discussions are reported.

Creative Writing

Writing projects give opportunity for class members to reinforce learning and become directly involved in the lesson by working through various creative writing activities. There are a variety of creative writing activities to choose from:

Letters—Writing letters makes the lesson come alive and makes it applicable. Letters may be written to the pastor, parents, a church leader, teacher, biblical character, or fictitious individual.

Articles, editorials, newspapers—Often class members work together on producing a "newspaper" or write articles and editorials. This aids greatly in learning Bible truths. Students develop headlines and articles on specific Bible stories or issues. Sometimes students spend several weeks working on such a newspaper project.

Stories—After telling a story to the class, students may display pictures, act out sections of the story, or report answers to specific questions. Teachers often use "open-ended stories." A story is told and the students are asked to write an ending to it. This is especially effective, even in adult classes, for encouraging life application.

Worksheets—Worksheets are a guide for researching lesson truths. Students study Scripture passages individually or in groups to determine answers to questions. Worksheets may also be used to determine student knowledge either before or after class.

Booklets—As a guide to learning the central truths of a particular lesson, students often develop a booklet incorporating information on a specific topic: for example, the steps of salvation, missionary journeys of Paul, steps of Bible study, or

Training When Meeting

Several years ago I met a preschool department teacher in a large church. During my observation of her class and later conversation with the teacher, I could see that she believed it was her responsibility to make the children sit still for the 45-minute Sunday school time. She didn't realize that what she was requiring these children to do was impossible to accomplish at their age. Her lack of understanding of preschool children resulted in an unhappy situation both for her and the children.

Most teachers sense a need to understand their students. Lately there have been many books written about student characteristics. At the end of this article you will find a brief description of the characteristics of each age group.

As with many of the articles in this booklet, the place to begin is in the Bible where we find Christ's principles for getting to know people.

Getting to Know Your Students

David E. Jenkins

Knowing Christ's Example

The Lord Jesus ministered to people of all types and age levels during his earthly experience. Some individuals were very close to him while others seemed to only pass through a situation to give us a picture of his concern for meeting their needs.

Christ knew the people to whom he ministered. It is clear in Luke 10 that Jesus felt it was important to spend time getting to know others. Martha was concerned about what she could *do for* Jesus, while Mary was concerned about *knowing* him. Jesus loved them both, but he pointed out that Mary had chosen the better part (v. 42).

Time is a key factor. The Lord spent three years with his disciples. There were occasions when Jesus took the disciples aside with him to rest and relax. As they retreated from specific ministries, they were able to be ministered to and be refreshed. The disciples observed Christ and benefited from seeing his life-style. He, in turn, saw the disciples in various situations and was able to meet them at their various points of need.

Knowing Begins With Careful Observation

If we are to teach the Word of God effectively, we must know our students' needs and how to build on what they already know in order to meet those needs. We must really know the students, not just think we know them.

Discover Your Students' Needs

Since students do not learn unless they sense a need to learn, discovering their needs is a vital area. Your teaching must be relevant. If you are teaching in one direction and the students have needs in another, you are not really helping them. As you evaluate your students' life-styles, belief patterns, and feelings about themselves, you can better adapt your teaching toward meeting their needs.

Find Out What Your Students Already Know

Students need to be exposed to a wide variety of Scripture. What would happen if your class studied only the book of Genesis? What happens if they hear the same material repeated over and over again? Younger age groups like and need repetition. However, if students know a Bible truth and are using it in their lives, you need to go on to something else. Don't be like a broken record; introduce your students to new truths. You can lead into new areas of learning only when you know where they have already been. Find out what they know and go on from there.

Begin to Meet Needs

Spiritual needs can be met as you seek to teach the Word of God and help students make personal applications. Meeting needs can be accomplished only when you take time to share concern and love for students. They will reveal needs as you let them know that you care.

Knowing Your Students Comes Through Involvement

As you get to know your students, you can begin to appreciate them. Knowing general characteristics is helpful, but that does not meet the entire need. Students must be known as individuals.

In Formal Class Situations

Because Sunday school is a structured learning situation, you can observe how they react in a formal class setting. Through using a variety of teaching methods involving student participation, you can determine what they know and what they still need to learn. You can observe how they seek to apply Bible truths to life. In the classroom you will also see what kind of relationships they have with their classmates.

Watch your students, ask them questions, and help them express themselves. This is an excellent way to learn about your students.

Privately and at Home

Times of close association are vital to a good relationship. Use any opportunity to talk with your students individually. Get to know who they are and what they think. Go for a walk with them, have lunch together— *listen.* Don't hurry. Building good relationships takes time.

Visiting your students in their homes will help you understand why they act and feel as they do. Notice relationships: parent to child, child to parent, and child to child. You will begin to identify needs just by observing their home environment.

During Fellowship Times

Just as it is important to observe your students in a formal situation, it is also important to see how they respond to each other in informal times. As you observe them, ask youself, "Are all students treated equally, or at least fairly?" "Is one person left out?" "Which students are most popular and why?" Again some general characteristics will surface, but as you watch your students, you will see many individual characteristics and needs as well.

Conclusion

People are valued highly by God. How can we do less than to know our students as important individuals for whom Christ died? Many people in our churches are hurting because no one seems to care enough to get to know them. You can make the difference as you break down barriers and get to *know your students.*

Characteristics of People at Every Age

I t is essential that you not only know the general characteristics of the age level you teach, but those of other age levels as well. This will help you to know where your students have been and how to prepare them for the future.

Preschoolers— Ages 2-5

Physically preschool children are small, but always growing, especially during the fourth and fifth years. Because their muscles are developing, they are restless and need lots of activity. As a result of this excessive activity they tire easily. Generally, they can do only one thing at a time and become frustrated when there are too

Preparing to Teach

Larry D. McCullough

Fruitful teaching results from intelligent planning. If you, as a Christian teacher, have planned and prepared adequately you will feel more confident in your presentation and can be assured of class participation and growth.

Preplanning Preparation

There are several stages to effective planning and preparation. The first two stages of preplanning involve personal preparation.

Study the Bible

In his book, *The Task of Christian Education,* D. Campbell Wyckoff raises this pertinent question, "How could one adopt and develop a Christian way of life without making the Bible his own, without seeking through all the days and years of his life to understand it, appreciate it, and come to the place where its truth and teachings are the very focus of his living?" Self-examination and personal Bible study begin a solid basis for good teaching. Not only is Bible study important for your own sake; it is important for the sake of those you teach. It is hard to lead others where you yourself have never been.

As you prepare to teach Bible lessons, choose a study method which involves more than just reading the passage. One of the following methods can help you do this:

1. Outline the passage in order to understand major points.
2. Answer these four questions:
   a. What does the passage say?
   b. What does the passage mean?
   c. How does the passage apply to contemporary life?
   d. What does the passage mean to me?
3. Respond to these three questions:
   a. What does God want me to KNOW from this passage?
   b. How does God want me to FEEL about the contents of this passage?
   c. What does God want me to DO in response to this passage?

For example, assume an upcoming lesson is dealing with the topic of how to handle fear and the main passage is Matt. 14:22-33. Fear is something everyone faces at some time in their lives. Think about your experiences with fear in the light of God's Word.

1. List things, people, and situations that cause you to become afraid or anxious.
2. How do these verses help you face fear: Ps. 34:4; Matt. 10:28; 14:22-33; Heb. 13:5, 6; and I John 4:4?
3. What barriers keep a person from overcoming fear? What is the solution to these barriers? Find Scripture verses that apply using a concordance.
4. Read Matt. 14:22-33 (the main passage). Is there any situation in your life that parallels that of Peter? Pray about it.

Personal, in-depth Bible study is a rewarding experience for every teacher and you need to plan in your schedule a specific time and guard that time as essential to your personal life and teaching experience.

Pray for Guidance

The second stage of personal preparation is prayer. Not only at the beginning but at each stage of your preparation earnestly ask God for his help and guidance. Pray for God's direction in applying the passage to your own life, determining the needs of your students and how the passage will meet them, and planning the teaching methods you will use to involve your students in the application of the Scripture passage.

Start your lesson preparation early. Some of the most effective teachers begin their preparation on the previous Sunday. Avoid the "Saturday Night Cramming Session." A well-taught lesson needs growing time.

Consider Students' Needs

The third stage of preplanning involves considering the needs of class members as they relate to the Scripture passage for the session. Quite often teachers become so concerned with teaching the points of the lesson that they forget the student is a whole person with many needs.

The emphasis of preparation is to discern the needs of the students and discover how a given Scripture passage can speak to those needs. The wise Bible teacher will set the stage for learning by recognizing and using the needs of the students to help them apply the truths of God's Word to their everyday concerns. Ask yourself, "In what ways does this passage speak to the needs of my class, and how can this lesson benefit my students this week?"

Define the Central Truth

We come now to the fourth stage of preplanning—defining or determining a central truth to be taught from a given Scripture passage. A central truth or specific focus is a theme from the Bible text on which you want your students to concentrate during the lesson. For example, if the Bible text is James 1:1-8, the focus may be in the area of handling trials. The central truth for this passage might be stated as "God's Principles for Handling Trials."

Every passage of Scripture contains at least one main idea. Once a specific focus for the lesson is chosen, you can use it as a guideline by which to design the Bible study. It is

better to choose one central truth and do a comprehensive job of covering that theme rather than selecting three or four themes and jumping from one to the other. Present the central message of the passage in a clear, brief sentence using the present tense.

Formulate Learning Aims

The fifth stage of preplanning is selecting learning aims for the lesson. Aims, sometimes referred to as objectives or goals, are simply a statement of exactly what the teacher wants to accomplish as a result of the session. Once you have the goal, you can easily choose the best road. There are basically three types of aims: the *informational* aim describes the facts to be learned; the *analytical* aim describes the meaning to be attached to those facts; the *personal* aim describes the application of the facts and their meanings in the students' lives. Each lesson can be planned to encourage specific steps of spiritual growth in the individual students.

In preparing a lesson, think of the capacity and interests of each of your students and make lesson plans to stimulate each to want to learn. The lesson aims should take into account the fact that the students are not all on the same intellectual and spiritual level and that their attainments and needs may differ widely. It is helpful for the aims to be stated in terms of the students' responses to the central truth as found in the Bible.

You should first study the Bible passage and the aims listed in the curriculum material. Then, using the printed aims as a guide, restate them to meet your students' needs.

Good planning aims should have the following three characteristics: *ownable* —students see the goal as

Training When Meeting

For centuries educators have been puzzled about the answer to this question. This discussion still goes on in educational institutions today, both Christian and secular. The purpose here is not to settle the question but to propose some principles by which you as a teacher can evaluate yourself.

As a Christian teacher the picture is a bit different from that of a teacher in secular education. Christian teachers need to keep two areas in mind when evaluating their teaching ministry: their spiritual growth, and the improvement of their teaching skills.

In Christian education, teaching skills cannot be divorced from the teacher's character. Being an effective teacher implies that the teacher not only embodies the truth himself, but that he is an effective communicator in the classroom as well.

Using the Lord Jesus as a model and as teachers come to identify with him more fully, depend upon him more completely, and learn of him more explicitly their ministry must become more effective.

The Teacher's Life —Committed to Christ

What did Paul mean when he wrote, "That the life of Jesus also may be manifested in our body"? Lives

What Makes Teachers Effective?

J. Omar Brubaker

are transformed to the likeness of Christ by God's work through the Spirit. But teachers can identify with him as students can identify with their teachers.

An appropriate illustration of what an effective teacher's life should reflect is found in John Bunyan's *Pilgrim's Progress.* After Pilgrim started on his way to the heavenly city and came by Interpreter's house, Interpreter (symbolic of the Holy Spirit) showed him a picture. It

is described this way: "Christian saw the picture of a very grave person hung up against the wall: and this was the fashion of it:

it had eyes lifted to heaven.
the best of books in its hand.
the law of truth was written upon its lips,
the world was behind its back:
it stood as if it pleaded with men, and a crown of gold did hang over its head."

Christian asked, "What meaneth this?"

Interpreter answered, "The man whose picture this is, is one of a thousand." (*Pilgrim's Progress,* (by John Bunyan. Universal Book and Bible House. Philadelphia, 1933.)

Although the writer meant that to be a picture of the ideal minister, it might also serve well as a picture of the ideal teacher.

Let's look at each of the statements from *Pilgrim's Progress* separately to illustrate the characteristics of an effective teacher's life.

A Person of PURPOSE-
"a very grave person"

You did not choose Me," Jesus said to his disciples, "but I chose you . . . that you should go and bear fruit, and that your fruit should remain." (John 15:16) Being called of God, and identified with Christ in this way, Christian teachers should desire to do their best for God and for their students. "For we do not preach ourselves, but Christ Jesus as Lord, and ourselves as your bond-servants for Jesus' sake." (II Cor. 4:5) How well do you measure up? Do you think of yourself in a servant's role?

A Person of PRAYER-
"eyes lifted to heaven"

In the morning, O Lord, Thou wilt hear my voice: In the morning I will order my prayer to Thee and eagerly watch." (Ps. 5:3) Jesus said, "Truly, truly, I say to you, the Son can do nothing of Himself." (John 5:19) Then He reminded his disciples, "apart from Me you can do nothing." (John 15:5) This tells us that all our efforts depend upon Christ for their effectiveness. Paul emphasizes this In II Cor. 3:5, "Not that we are adequate in ourselves to consider anything as coming from ourselves, but our adequacy is from God." The teacher's prayer life reflects his degree of dependency upon God. What does your prayer life reflect?

A Person of THE WORD-*"the best of books in its hand"*

Let the word of Christ richly dwell within you." Paul wrote to the Colossians, "with all wisdom teaching and admonishing one another with psalms and hymns and spiritual songs." (Col. 3:16) Unless the Word of God grasps the teacher, he cannot expect it to grasp his students. Jeremiah, Job, and David are examples of those whose desire for the Word was keen. (Jer. 15:16; Job 23:12; Ps. 19:10, 11) Paul's admonition is equally timeless. "Be diligent to present yourselves approved to God as a workman who does not need to be ashamed, handling accurately the word of truth." (II Tim. 2:15) As the Word dwells richly within teachers, the Word within them becomes "spirit" and "life" to their hearers.

How much do you desire the Word of God? Do your students see a genuine love for the Bible reflected in your actions and words?

A Person of WITNESS-
"the law of truth written upon its lips"

Think of how Paul effectively communicated the Word. "But we proved to be gentle among you, as a nursing mother tenderly cares for her own children." And, "Just as you know how we were exhorting and encouraging and imploring each one of you as a father would his own children." (I Thess. 2:7, 11) Peter speaks of being ready to share with "everyone who asks you . . . the hope that is in you, yet with gentleness and reverence." (I Peter 3:15) You have this challenging opportunity as a teacher to share the hope that is in you—the love of Jesus. How effective are you in sharing the gospel with your students?

A Person SEPARATED from the World-*"the world was behind its back"*

Separation may be legalistic, self-righteous, or a monk-like withdrawing from society. However, you can exemplify a separation of love—as a bride to the groom. The world is behind your back because you are following Jesus, and you are deeply in love with him. "Do not love the world, nor the things in the world. If anyone loves the world, the love of the Father is not in him." (I John 2:15) Your positive example will teach volumes. How's your separation from the world?

A Person of PASSION-*"it stood as if it pleaded with men"*

A deep concern for the salvation of sinners and the spiritual growth of believers should characterize the Christian teacher. Paul writes of it in terms of a pleading ambassador. "Therefore, we are ambassadors for Christ, as though God were entreating through us; we beg you on behalf of Christ, be reconciled to God." (II Cor. 5:20) It is not enough to come to the Savior, but "we are to grow up in all aspects unto Him." (Eph. 4:15) Paul expresses his personal concern for Galatian converts: "My children, with whom I am again in labor until Christ is formed in you." (Gal. 4:19)

It should almost go without saying that the Christian teacher should desire to have his students become Christians. Some feel that their job is finished when their students accept Christ as Savior. But teachers should desire that their students grow up in Him.

Are you really concerned about reaching your unsaved students? Do you seek to have each student grow up in the faith?

The Teacher's Ministry— Controlled by Christ

Having seen the picture of the ideal Christian teacher, it is necessary to look at the teacher's ministry for the two are inseparable.

Richardson wrote in his book *The Christ of the Classroom,* "The supreme glory of the teaching profession consists on the fact that when Jesus Christ faced his life work, he chose to be a teacher."

The master Teacher had a clearly defined life purpose as well as goals for his ministry. Christian teachers need also to clarify their own reasons for teaching, their personal attitudes, and their goals for their students.

Clarifying Purpose

For yourself-Do you reflect a positive attitude about yourself in the classroom: a sense of personal adequacy? This involves personal acceptance, self-esteem, and confidence. As you confidently accept yourself as the very special person that you are and that God made you, your ability to be open and sharing is enhanced. Being yourself—natural, positive, and casual makes it easy for the students to accept and respect you.

Enthusiasm in your teaching and specific attitudes are important dynamics in the classroom. Your students will observe how you feel about them, yourself, your job as a teacher, and the Lord and his Word. These feelings will be positive and exemplary if Christ is living through you.

For your students—You can help your students develop self-esteem. Provide opportunities for them to participate in meaningful ways. Guide them in developing positive attitudes towards others, the learning situation, yourself as a teacher, and the Lord and his Word.

Accept students where they are and lead them toward their true potential. Seek to develop in them a love for the Lord and his Word and a desire to know and to do his will. Guide them in Bible exploration and study to learn directly from God's Word. Help them find answers to their questions and needs. Encourage them to apply the truth "here and now."

For your lessons—A specific aim helps to target each lesson. Learn to know your students well so you can formulate aims in light of their personal needs.

Depending on God

The teacher's life should be a model of prayer and dependence upon God. Students can catch your example of reverence in the departmental and class worship.

The Holy Spirit—The Christian educator's version of Zech. 4:6 reads, "It's not by the might of excellent methods, nor by the power of polished techniques, but by my spirit, saith the Lord."

Study the work of the Holy Spirit in the teaching-learning situation. Help your students learn about the Holy Spirit and his ministry to them.

Prayer—The teacher's practice of prayer should involve more than "God bless my class." Here are some suggestions for making prayers more meaningful:

Pray for yourself.

Pray over your study of the Scriptures.

Pray for individuals in your class and their specific needs.

Pray for guidance in choosing methods and applications.

Pray for the work of the Holy Spirit in your life and the lives of your students.

Prayer in the classroom should be personal, meaningful, and effective. It should involve your students. Let them say with Jesus' disciples, "Teach us to pray." An attitude of reverence and expectancy should underlie the atmosphere of each classroom session. Students need to sense and feel the presence of God.

Teaching With Authority

Christian teachers are charged with "handling accurately the Word of truth." (II Tim. 2:15)

Under authority—The Christian teacher's authority is the Lord himself, and God's Word. He is responsible to submit to God, allowing the Holy Spirit to control the teaching situation. He can have confidence because he does not speak from his own ideas.

The use of the Word—Recognize that the Bible is the textbook of Christian education, and give priority to personal Bible study in lesson preparation. Here are some tips which reinforce the important place of the Bible in teaching:

Teach from an open Bible, not a teacher's guide. Use the Bible, and encourage students to use theirs. Provide Bibles when they are needed for students who did not bring their own. Appeal to

the Scriptures; encourage students to find out what the Bible says about the lesson topic. Help your students to learn how to study the Bible for themselves.

If your students have difficulty using the Bible in class it is a good indication that they aren't using it on their own.

Provide variety in the use of the Bible and Scripture reading in the classroom. Here are some ideas to provide variety: Use different translations whenever appropriate; read in unison, responsively, or individually; have students read silently then give the verse in their own words; let individuals take the part of a character and "role read"; read background sections yourself and have students read the key passages.

Memorizing Scripture is an important part of the teaching process. A teacher can lend a note of authority in teaching by simply quoting a verse or passage appropriately. Encourage students to memorize the Word. Some tips for teaching the key, or special verse of the lesson are: take it seriously—memorize the verse yourself; visualize the verse for your students; introduce it early in the lesson and refer to it often during the lesson; teach students how to use it in life situations; help younger students memorize the verse using a memory game; repeat the verse when reviewing the entire lesson; do not stress rote memory; expect the class to memorize and they will.

Sharpening Communication Skills

Teachers often confuse telling with teaching and listening with learning. To communicate effectively you must: start where the student is; remember that learning is based on interest and need; teach in light of learning being an active process; view it as a continuing process; and expect that it takes place through identification. In essence, learning is an inner process; it takes place in the lives of your students. It has been said "Teachers have not taught until their class members have begun to live." Learning results in changed attitudes and conduct.

Improving teaching skills involves the teacher, but in the process the student is helped. The effective teacher will use a variety of both impressional and expressional methods. The teacher is primarily the active participant in impressional methods while the student is the active participant in expressional methods. Some examples of impressional methods are: lecture, storytelling, memorization, and testing. Expressional activities might include: group projects, instructive play, role playing, and group activity.

Motivation to improve may come through self or other evaluation: observing others teach; learning of new approaches and skills; reading; attending workshops or seminars; or personal supervision.

Sharing Convictions

Students will soon learn what a teacher's priorities are. They can easily sense what you feel deeply about. C.S. Lewis said, "Some ideas are communicated more forcefully if gently assumed rather than actively taught." This would include such attitudes as love for God and his Word.

Showing Concern

Salvation emphasis in teaching—Evangelism is the teacher's constant concern. However, a steady diet of evangelism is not sufficient to feed those who need to grow in the Lord. When the lesson presents a strong salvation emphasis, the believing students need to be challenged as to how they could use the Bible portion in sharing the plan of salvation with a friend.

Here are some suggestions regarding the salvation emphasis:

Pray much, depend on the Holy Spirit for results. Present the message tactfully, naturally, and appropriately. Use the Bible. Provide for opportunity to privately counsel students who respond to an invitation. Avoid symbolism with young children—make sure you understand any symbols used. Do not assume that students are saved—check with them personally. Use some variety in salvation emphasis and appeals. Reach some unsaved students on a personal basis outside of class. Follow-up absentees; they are often unsaved.

Christian growth and discipleship—How can the teacher train those who have been won in discipleship, and encourage the spiritual growth of all the class members? Here are some suggestions:

Help every student to study the Bible himself.

Teach students to have meaningful devotions.

Help students to learn how to share their faith.

Encourage them to practice what they learn.

Spend time with them outside of class.

Consider extra study sessions for students who want to study a subject more in-depth.

Pray together; encourage personal requests for prayer.

Give students opportunity for expression, practice, and leadership.

Encourage spiritually mature students to help those less-advanced.

Conclusion

Remember the illustration from *Pilgrim's Progress* at the beginning of this study? "A crown of gold did hang over its head." Interpreter said, "that is to show thee that, slighting and despising the things that are present, for the love that he hath to his Master's service, he is sure in the world that comes next to

have glory for his reward.

Interpreter added, "I have showed thee this picture first because the man whose picture this is, is the only man whom the Lord of the place whither thou are going hath authorized to be thy guide. . . ."

You can be such a guide.

You can be "one of a thousand."

Rev. J. Omar Brubaker is a member of the Christian education faculty at Moody Bible Institute in Chicago.

Review Questions

1. Why can't teaching skills be divorced from the character of the teacher?
2. How can a teacher become more effective by identifying more closely with Jesus?
3. How could you improve the practice of prayer in your own life as well as in the lives of your students?
4. What are the best methods for presenting the plan of salvation in the classroom?
5. What hinders students from becoming more mature in the faith after accepting Christ as Savior?

Application Activities

1. Write your own definition of learning. Make a list of ways learning could be improved in your classroom.
2. Make a study of how Jeremiah, Job, and David desired the Word of God and decide how you could better reflect their attitude toward the Bible.
3. Make a list of the ways Jesus remained "in the world" but still separated from it. Seek to apply these principles to your lifestyle.

worthwhile to work toward; *reachable*—students see it as realistic and able to be accomplished; *measurable* —students can know when it has been completed.

It takes time and effort to discover effective learning aims. One would not think of building a house without a set of blueprints. Similarly, building a successful lesson which leads to spiritual growth in your students depends on specific ownable, reachable, and measurable aims.

Provide for Total-session Teaching Strategy

Teaching/learning philosophy —Before actually preparing a lesson, it is helpful to understand the impact of your personal teaching/learning philosophy. Are you more concerned with getting your students into the Bible or getting the Bible into your students? There will be a difference in the result. Getting your students into the Bible will increase their abilities to remember facts and principles revealed in God's Word. Getting the Bible into your students internalizes God's truth to the point the biblical principles become a part of their life-styles. It is strongly suggested that students be encouraged to examine Scripture and to discover God's truths and principles for themselves.

There is an old saying that, "If you give a boy a fish, he will eat for a day. Teach a boy to fish, and he will eat for a lifetime." Instead of spoon-feeding your class members, encourage them to dig into the Bible to make first-hand discoveries about what God's Word says and means. Once the passage has been explored and application has been made, each student can decide specifically how he plans to use the principle in his daily life.

II Tim. 3:14-16 and James 1:22 point to the fact that the purpose of Bible study is changed lives. Your goal as a teacher should be to assist and guide students of any age to explore God's Word and make progressive, positive life changes through the power of the Holy Spirit. This will lead to spiritual maturity.

Teaching Methods—The selection of appropriate methods and activities is important in helping students know, appreciate, and apply the principles and truths of God's Word. The primary goals are student interaction with the truths in God's Word and a positive permanent effect on the students' attitudes and lives. Methods are only the means to achieving positive learning and active application. Do not select methods at random without purpose; select methods that will help you achieve these learning goals. These methods are strategic learning tools by which your students will better retain and apply the principles of the lesson.

Wise teachers provide a variety of creative Bible learning strategies that involve the students in purposeful Bible study. People learn not only what they hear, but also what they see, feel, smell, say, and, most significantly, do. Limiting the message to only the hearing channel of learning is narrowing the learning potential of the individual students. Session four in this booklet provides additional insights on involving students in the lesson.

Lesson Organization —Every effective class session includes three main parts:

Approach—The effectiveness of any class session is greatly increased when the teacher draws his listeners into the subject matter at the very beginning. An approach activity captures the students' interest, introduces the theme in an inviting way, and helps the students focus their attention on that theme. An approach activity can be as simple as a question, or as involved as a brief creative assignment.

Bible Exploration—During the Bible exploration time, choose various teaching methods to help students explore what the Bible says and apply its truths to their lives. Class members need to identify God's principles and how they relate to contemporary living.

Conclusion/decision—This section is a practical way of helping the students decide, "What am I going to do with the material that has been presented?" It is a specific method designed to evoke personal response in each student. A conclusion/ decision activity may range from a brief prayer in pairs or threes, to a specific project based on the session's theme, which is to be followed-up during the succeeding week.

Make up a session plan worksheet for you to use in preparation for your next teaching session. . Write your initial ideas in a column labeled Pre-Plan Ideas. If you are planning alone, make a final decision of what to do and write your ideas in a column labeled Final Plan. If you teach with a team, make final selections at a team planning meeting and list those ideas on the plan sheet. Make note of any materials or

supplies needed for the lesson. It is also helpful to plot out time allotments for each major part of the lesson.

Post-planning Preparation

No matter what the Scripture passage is or what teaching methods are selected, thorough planning greatly enhances your teaching. After your plans are completed, there are some post-planning steps you need to take. Prepare your notes and any visuals or materials that will be included in the lesson. Schedule for the use of any equipment and contact helpers or special speakers to remind them. Plan to be early so you have plenty of time to set up the room. Above all, pray, pray, pray—and get a good night's sleep.

Conclusion

Today, you as a Christian educator, ought to be able to do a better job of teaching the Bible than ever before. Better facilities, better equipment, and better curriculum are available. You need to make the most of your opportunities as teachers by striving for excellence instead of settling for mediocrity. The result of your dedication and desire for continual growth should result in new life for your Sunday school classes and changed lives among those for whom God has given you responsibility.

Dr. Larry D. McCullough is the Director of Biblical Education by Extension and professor of Christian Education at Columbia Bible College, Columbia, South Carolina. He is also a member of the Board of Directors of the Evangelical Teacher Training Association.

Review Questions

Answer the following questions from the article.
1. Why is it important to spend time in prayer and personal Bible study before you prepare the actual lesson?
2. Explain the three characteristics of good planning/learning aims.
3. Why is it important that your students make first-hand discoveries in the Bible?
4. State one of the primary goals which you as a teacher should have for your students.
5. Explain the characteristics and importance of a good approach activity.
6. Define the following items: central truth, aims, approach, conclusion/decision.

Application Activities

1. A. If you are using prepared curriculum for your lessons, evaluate the aims for the next lesson. Does each aim relate directly to the central truth for the passage? Is each aim ownable, reachable, measurable? Rewrite any aims that do not meet the standards.
   B. If your curriculum does not specify aims, read over the Scripture and the teacher's guide and write your central truth and aims.
   C. If you use only the Bible in preparation, study the passage and complete the last part of B above.
2. A. Make a list of changes or improvements you want to make in your lesson preparation procedure.
   B. Identify one change or improvement you want to begin working on right away.
   C. Write a note to God asking for his help in completing this goal.

many options available to them. Learning, for preschool children particularly, requires the involvement of all their senses.

Mentally preschoolers have a limited vocabulary. At age two their vocabulary may be only a few hundred words; however, by the end of their fifth year it may be over 1000 words. The attention span of preschool children is short, usually ranging from three to six minutes per activity.

Variety is essential in order to meet preschoolers' needs. They cannot just sit down, listen, and learn. They are literal in their thinking patterns, and their minds are not yet able to comprehend symbolism. Preschool children learn by observing other people, by asking questions, and by using their senses.

Socially they are unique persons. Children in this age bracket are usually very self-centered (not to be equated with being selfish). In their early years they play *alongside* other children. As they get older they begin to make friends more easily and will play *with* others.

Emotionally they are growing and expanding. In these early years they need to feel a strong sense of security. They have many fears, especially of new situations and places. If things do not go as they want, preschoolers show anger. Their world revolves around themselves, but as they develop they become more able to express a caring attitude toward others.

Spiritually preschoolers want to know about God. Although they have a very limited ability to understand spiritual concepts, they can begin to trust in God. As they grow, they will begin to think of God in some very personal ways, such as: "God loves me, and God cares."

Primaries— Ages 6-8

Physically primary children are going through many changes. They grow at a different rate from their peers—some children develop rapidly while others have a growth spurt later. Because their muscles are maturing and need to be used, they are generally active.

Mentally primary children can quickly move into the world of make-believe. Reading and writing are new adventures for them, and they need to regularly practice both skills. Their attention span is longer. They can usually work with an activity for about 15 to 20 minutes. Primaries are curious and enjoy exploring new things.

Socially primary children are changing. They are inclined to play well with children of both sexes. Primaries want to have friends and enjoy being with them. They do not like to be considered "little" even though they are small in stature.

Emotionally primary children are often shy and find it difficult to express themselves. Many times they are fearful of new situations. They like things done when and how they want.

Spiritually primary children often are ready to accept Christ as Savior. They find it easy to believe that God can and does answer prayer. Generally, they have many questions about heaven such as: "Where is it?" and "What is it like?"

Juniors—Ages 9-11

Juniors are quite different from any of the children discussed to this point. There are some major changes in each of the five areas of discussion.

Physically they are extremely active and competitive. Because their coordination skills are developing, they like the challenge of difficult activities. Along with all of their activity they like to make noise.

At this age, girls are usually bigger and more developed than boys.

Mentally juniors are inquisitive. They want to see how (but not necessarily why) things work. Although they are beginning to put facts together and come to a conclusion, this ability will be better refined in the next few years. They enjoy reading and writing and desire to use these acquired skills.

Socially they like to take on jobs which give them a sense of responsibility. They thrive on the "gang" or "club" spirit. They are very much aware of how others feel about them. They want to look up to someone as a model or hero.

Emotions are difficult for juniors to control at times. They may explode with anger or express disappointment very easily. Boys, in particular, do not like affection shown openly.

Spiritually they have a great potential for growth. They may have many questions about what they are supposed to believe. Even though they desire to know God, they will need constant encouragement. Juniors may make a spiritual decision and not show any emotion. Juniors have the capacity to distinguish good from evil, but need the positive example of others to provide a good model.

Young Teens— Ages 12-13

Young teens are their own unique breed. They are one of the most challenging groups to work with and one of the most rewarding. The only consistent thing about young teens is their inconsistency!

Physically young teens are in one of the major growth periods of their lives. Because of this fast growth they are often awkward. During this period girls usually develop faster than boys.

Young teens often have ravenous appetites and seem to be hungry all the time. Because they are growing and changing so rapidly, they sometimes become fatigued quickly.

Mentally young teens generally progress very well. They are capable of doing some quality thinking. However, they many times will prejudge a situation. They enjoy learning activities which require them to discover truth on their own.

Socially young teens want to make their own decisions. They see this as important in realizing their desire to be recognized as adults. The "group" is very important, and they must have a sense of belonging. The peer pressure to do what the group does is almost staggering. Teens are pressured to do things they usually would not do in order to prove that they are part of the gang. Because of all the physiological and psychological changes young teens are experiencing, they are concerned about how others feel.

Emotionally young teens are in a state of upheaval. Their emotions vacillate constantly. Often the change is quite drastic. They may hold you in highest regard at one moment and show you disrespect the next. Many times they think people do not understand them. This is probably true, but they don't understand themselves either. Their emotions are very strong and they sometimes have little or no control over them.

Spiritually young teens want faith to be practical. They have established high standards for their Christianity and may expect perfection from others. Although they may develop many doubts along the way, they can be encouraged to follow Christ. Though they may face times of frustration or times when they don't understand things, they still are interested in helping people through various service projects.

Older Teens— Ages 14-17

As teens move through the last years of their "youth experience" they begin to complete the foundation from which they will enter adulthood.

Physically they are still growing; however, they are becoming stronger and taking on more mature features. Older teens are able to cope with constant activity more than at any other time in their lives.

Mentally older teens are alert. They seek to think through processes before making any judgment. They are deciding what to do in the future. Questions such as: "Should I go to college, technical school, or get a job?" and "What does the future hold?" are going through their minds. Because of their capability to think and reason, they are now experiencing a new sense of freedom.

Socially they are attracted to people who share their interests. They usually seek to be friendly although at times may feel insecure. Older teens want to be popular; therefore, they seek to develop interests in many areas.

Emotionally they have had several years to develop confidence and experience. They can usually control their emotions. Because they fear very few things, they are willing to try almost anything once.

Spiritually older teens are concerned about their personal relationship with Jesus Christ. However, they sometimes find commitment to anything difficult. They want their faith to be realistic so they can share it with others.

Adults—Ages 18 and Older

Because of the wide age range, the adult area is quite complex. Therefore, no attempt will be made to cover the five areas of characteristics for them. Rather, some general information regarding adults will be given.

The adult years comprise the longest period in a person's life. These years are characterized by important decisions, productivity, and several crises.

For many, *young adult life* begins with the breaking away from home and the psychological security found there. At this age, decisions concerning a lifetime career, future life-style, and the formation of their own families are uppermost in young adults' priorities.

Middle adulthood brings a period of continuing, developing, maturing, and deepening. These years are characterized by: establishing and maintaining a standard of living; raising children; relating to spouses; coping with the physiological changes of middle age; adjusting to aging parents.

Later adulthood comprises for many the retirement years. Older adults are faced with these adjustments: decreased physical health and strength; reduced retirement income; explicit identification with their age group; satisfactory physical living arrangements.

Teachers working with adults at any stage of development need to recognize the circumstances facing the individuals in their classes and find ways to effectively minister to their needs.

David Jenkins is a member of the Christian Education faculty of Grace College of the Bible in Omaha, Nebraska.

Review Questions

1. What five major areas should be considered when developing student characteristics?
2. How did Jesus get to know people?
3. Why is it important to observe and listen to students?
4. Why is it necessary to know your students well?
5. How can teachers get to know their students better?

Application Activities

1. Describe each of your students in detail, using five major characteristic divisions.
2. Study the relationship of Jesus with his disciples to see how you might better know your students.

principles of parenting.

Poems—Some are better than others with poetry but all can create a basic rhyme. Groups or individuals may summarize a basic lesson theme through writing a poem. Since further information is often necessary for writing the poem, study and research result.

Bible paraphrase—Paraphrasing, putting a Bible passage into one's own words, is perhaps the best means of summarizing the meaning of a passage. It is only possible, however, after study has clarified the meaning. This may be done either individually, in small groups, or as a class.

Written prayers—Commitment to God is perhaps the most essential step in teaching his truth. Asking each student to write a prayer to God at the conclusion of class encourages the crystallization of lesson truths.

Music

Music is a very enjoyable medium. But, music is also a useful learning technique. It may be used for teaching in several ways:

Learning a song—Christ-glorifying songs have a great potential for enriching learning. Teachers may select songs emphasizing lesson themes and teach the song each week to highlight lesson truths. This also encourages and develops musical abilities to be used for God's glory.

Musical background—The background of a particular song is not only interesting but also gives added significance to the words, thus increasing learning.

Writing a song—Few people have the ability to compose songs. Those who do should be encouraged to write a song related to the lesson theme. Most, however, are able to write new words to familiar tunes. An effective learning activity, therefore, is for students to write words correlated with a familiar tune.

Art

Everyone enjoys art activities. Art also can be used to enhance and solidify learning. Consider the variety of art activities for use in learning:

Newspaper/Magazine clippings—Newspapers and magazines often illustrate either the positive or negative side of lesson themes. Students may select clippings from newspapers or magazines either prior to classtime or as an in-class activity to illustrate lesson truths.

Collage—A popular art activity is to make a collage of pictures. Pictures, headlines, articles are displayed on a board to illustrate a particular concept or truth. Students are able to contemplate lesson truths as they work on the collage.

Drawings/Pictures—Bible content and life application can be reinforced and taught as students produce drawings and pictures. This activity has been used successfully in adult classes as well as with children. An expanded version of drawings or pictures is the mural/frieze in which several feet of paper are used. The entire class often makes the mural, many times telling the entire Bible story. This may also be used for diagramming a Bible passage or scriptural concepts.

Diagrams—Since Paul often wrote in a logical, systematic sequence, further understanding of many Pauline passages is enhanced with drawing a diagram depicting the relationship of the thoughts to each other. Diagrams also are used to illustrate biblical relationships.

Mobiles—A mobile is an arrangement of thin forms suspended in mid-air by fine wires. It is often effective when lesson truths involve a variety of thoughts.

Drama

No student should be coerced into drama activities, but opportunity for involvement should be given. Often non-threatening dramatic methods can be used in which all can participate. The use of drama in teaching will be discussed in session six of *Training When Meeting.*

Formal Class

Student participation is not limited to small group and individual activity; students can be actively involved while remaining in the formal structure of the class setting. Although semi-circular room settings are best, rows of chairs do not prevent student involvement. Many adults are more willing to participate if they can remain in the traditional class setting. The teacher's creativity is the only limiting factor in involving students.

The following are only a few possibilities:

Panels—Experts on a particular subject may be asked to serve on a panel. The teacher asks several questions and then allows class members to question the panel. Sometimes the questions are determined by the class prior to panel presentation. Often "non-expert" class members rotate serving on the panel giving opportunity for sharing ideas.

Debates—Scriptural truths often involve a variety of opinions or interpretations. A debate is a good way to positively present both positions. Debaters need to be enlisted prior to class so they can prepare their case. The debate may be followed by a summary of the points of both positions and further questions and discussion.

Listing/brainstorming—Students are asked to list all possible answers to a question. Each answer is accepted and often recorded on a visual aid. This activity may also be used in small groups but is effective in the full class also.

Agree/disagree—In this activity a series of statements is

presented and students are asked if they agree or disagree. This may be signified by raising hands, standing up, or even moving to one side of the room. These statements are then used as the basis for further Bible study and discussion.

Case study—Particular situations are shared with the class members and they then suggest various solutions to the situation.

Question/Answer, Discussion—These are among the most popular methods for class involvement, especially with adults. The problem, of course, is that they involve only a minimum of the class members. Discussion questions have no *one* answer and usually involve "opinion topics."

Question/answer are more factual, making an attempt to involve class members in learning scriptural truths. These methods are often combined with small group activities.

Reverse roles—In this activity, a discussion/debate takes place with half of the students supporting one position and half supporting the other position. At the mid-point of the discussion, the class members switch sides and support the opposing position. This is very helpful in allowing class members to understand both positions or interpretations of a Bible passage.

Scripture search—The teacher has the class members search their Bibles for answers to specific questions or passages which deal with particular topics. This may be done individually, in small groups, or as an entire class.

Principles for Involving Students

Wise teachers will use as many ideas as possible to involve students in the learning process. In the use of these ideas, several basic principles should be followed.

Determine Lesson Objectives

Each part of a lesson should aid in accomplishing the stated objectives. Therefore, the first step in planning student involvement is to determine lesson aims. Don't have activity for the sake of activity. Objectives provide the basis for class involvement which will best accomplish the purposes of the lesson.

Match Activities to Objectives

The purpose of student-involvement learning activities is not primarily activity but learning. Once the lesson objectives have been stated, the teacher must determine the activities and other means of student involvement which will best accomplish the objectives. The most pertinent question is "Will this technique or method help the students to learn the lesson?"

Start Slowly

It is often difficult for students to adjust to class involvement if they are used to listening to a teacher presentation or participating in a general class discussion. This is especially true in adult classes. In these cases, it is best to start slowly. Keep the same general format and periodically add opportunities for student involvement.

Provide for Variety

Using the identical involvement technique each week can be as monotonous as no student involvement at all. Seek to vary the methods used for involving students in the lesson. Many classes, particularly those with more than one teacher, provide a choice of involvement activities. To help establish variety, the teacher can keep track of methods used to determine if various activities are being utilized.

Conclusion

Effective teaching depends upon student involvement. A wise teacher will make it a significant part of each lesson. A departmental superintendent visited a children's class one morning and found groups of children in varied activities: drawing a picture of a Bible story, preparing to put on a play, making a newspaper. He said to the teacher, "Isn't there any teaching going on here?" The teacher responded, "No, but there's an awful lot of learning going on!" May this be true in many classes as teachers learn and use new ways to involve students.

Rev. Paul J. Loth is the Director of the certificate, demoninational, and higher education programs at the Evangelical Teacher Training Association.

Review Questions

1. Give examples of a class you participated in where all activity was teacher-centered.
2. Give an example of a class you participated in where activities were student-centered.
3. You are talking to a teacher who does not see the need to involve his students—how would you explain to him the importance of student involvement?
4. List what you consider to be the five most effective ways to involve students.

Application Activities

1. Visit a class in which students are involved and observe methods used and how they result in the five reasons for student involvement.
2. Read through the lesson plans in your teacher's guide for the next month and list the methods suggested for student involvement. If these are limited, develop some additional activities you would plan to use.

entire program of pertinent data.

A good question has great value as a means of review. Does last week's lesson tie into this week's? Ask some pointed questions about last week's lesson. Much of the old material will come flooding back into the minds of your students.

For You as a Teacher

A good question will help you to establish rapport with your students. By asking someone something, you automatically imply that you believe the person is capable of answering. Express your confidence in your students through your questions.

A question reveals the level of your students' understanding, and the way they answer can suggest how to help them.

A good question will help you as a teacher to keep in contact with the minds of your students. Through whatever means, information can and does get falsely communicated. If your students have somehow gained some misinformation, a well-aimed question will quickly bring this to light.

A good question is one of the few ways to test classroom instruction. There is no better tool in evaluating the effectiveness of your teaching.

Characteristics of Good Questions

Good questions are characterized by a number of factors. They are:

Brief

A long-winded question becomes confusing—the student isn't sure what the heart of the question really is. Work at communicating the essence of a question in a few words.

Clear

The student should have enough of a problem answering the question—without having first to answer: "Now what is the teacher actually asking?" Use precise words. Steer clear of muddy, catch-all phrases.

Thought-provoking

Try to ask questions that the students had not thought of before. New problems are always interesting—especially if they are made relevant to the lives of the students.

Accommodating

Adapt questions to the level of knowledge and experience of your students. You might ask a new Christian: "Why are you as a Christian sinless in God's sight?" instead of, "Can you define justification?"

Forward-looking

A queston should be constructed so as to prepare for future study on the part of the students. It will open new vistas of thinking to explore. It will lead into the material planned for later in the class discussion.

Involving

A good question requires a personal interaction with the material. There are three things to remember here:

A good question will not suggest its answer. When the tempting lawyer asked Jesus what he must do to inherit eternal life, Jesus responded by asking: "What is written in the law? How readest thou?" This technique required that the lawyer creatively interact with what was in the law—the material. Had Jesus asked: "What does the law say about loving God and men?" the lawyer could have taken his cue for the answer right from the question.

Usually a good question will have more than two possible answers. Simple questions with either/or answers give even the daydreamer a fifty-fifty chance of answering correctly.

The same applies for mere yes-or-no-answer questions. In most cases, such questions contain a hint of whether the answer is negative or affirmative—and are too easy to cause student interaction with the material.

Informative

Whenever possible, include the source of information within the question itself. For example, you might ask: "What things do we learn about Christ from the first five verses of John 1?" By this device, a student is directed to John 1 as a source of information about Christ.

Original

The easy way out is to ask a question in the words of the text. But this leaves the student free to answer in the words of the text (if he has read it). The responsibility of the teacher is to creatively relate the material to the problems and interest of the students.

Logical

The question should make good sense. It should rest in the context of what has gone immediately before. Don't try to bend the material to produce a truth you want to put across. Ask questions which are natural to the intended sense of the passage you are studying.

Purposeful

Don't ask questions merely to

fill time. Each question should have one or more purposes. And these purposes can range from getting the attention of someone who isn't listening to determining how well the lesson content has been grasped.

Techniques for Using Questions

There are many techniques which can help you use questions more effectively. Knowing the technique available, you as teacher will be able to choose the most appropriate at any given moment in a classroom situation.

Ask the Whole Class

Don't name a student, then ask the question. For example: "Tom, can you tell us about the general subject-matter of the first four commandments?" In such a case, all ears except Tom's may turn off. A better method is to ask the question of the entire class.

Be Conversational

Avoid a stilted presentation of questions. A relaxed and natural-sounding question will get a more spontaneous answer. Informality puts students at ease, and creates a better atmosphere for thinking through to an answer.

Distribute Your Questions

The tendency in any class is for two or three to dominate by answering the majority of the questions. Try to get responses to questions from a good cross-section of the class. If you feel a student has given an incomplete answer, you might ask the other class members if they have anything more to add.

Allow Time for the Answer

You must be sensitive here. Don't give students a rushed "answer-right-now-or-else" feeling. If it seems that the students are making mental progress on the answer, give the few extra seconds they may need to formulate that answer into words.

Don't Over-question

A teacher is still responsible to communicate a certain amount of material. Don't rely on questions to the point of shortchanging your students' involvement in other learning activities. Jesus used questions extensively, yet his ministry shows that he did not rely on questions to the exclusion of other methods of teaching.

Be Self-critical

Examine the questions you use in light of the points contained in this article. Ask what your purposes are behind the questions. Don't assume that any interrogative sentence you use is necessarily a good teaching question.

Be Helpful

Never ask questions in such a manner as to imply: "See how much more I know about this subject than you?" Always ask your questions to help your students come into a greater understanding of God's Word, and his plan for their lives.

Hugh M. Salisbury is a member of the Christian education faculty at Multnomah School of the Bible in Portland, Oregon. Information in this article is adapted from Mr. Salisbury's book A Guide to Effective Bible Teaching and is used with his permission.

Review Questions

1. Why are questions so important in your teaching ministry?
2. In what ways have your questions in class failed to measure up to the points in this article?
3. In what ways have your questions successfully measured up?
4. List five important factors to keep in mind while framing questions for use in class.
5. What is the single most valuable lesson you learned in this session?

Application Activities

1. Visit a fellow teacher's class to see how he uses questions during his class session. Take notes and discuss your observations with him after class.
2. Look through a lesson in a teacher's guide used in your educational program. Using the principles mentioned in this article, evaluate and/or formulate some questions that could be used when teaching the lesson.

the same time. Use pantomime, rhythm games, and finger plays first, to prepare children for the use of dialogue later.

Children also need opportunity for plenty of large-muscle activity. This allows them to learn by moving and experiencing, the way in which they learn most effectively. However, very active, physically-taxing dramatic methods should be used only for short periods with young children.

It is not enough for children to hear God's Word, or even to memorize it. They must be given opportunities to *do* God's Word. Although they are unable to grasp abstractions, young children can learn God's truth if the activities are brief and simple, containing concrete and tangible Bible truths. Dramatization helps children learn these truths by the means God himself designed into each child's learning process.

Drama with Youth

There is a variety of dramatic possibilities for use with youth. Action-filled lessons appeal to their sense of excitement; physically-taxing methods take advantage of their physical capabilities. They are able to put themselves into the situations of Bible characters and can portray the emotions involved. With their capability for abstract thinking, symbolic forms of dramatization can be enlightening to them. The wise teacher will use dramatization to make the Bible lesson come alive. Again, drama can take full advantage of the abilities given to each student by God himself.

Drama with Adults

Some adults may be reluctant to try learning methods which are new and different. When working with a group of adults who are not accustomed to drama, it is best to begin with simple, non-threatening dramatizations. Adults will be more willing to become involved at first in a simple dialogue or two-person role play than in a drama where a great deal of physical action is required. The teacher will find it helpful to personally demonstrate a dramatization before asking his adult students to participate.

Adults are able to understand complex concepts and truths. Older adults whose physical situation prohibits physically-taxing dramatic forms may be willing to participate in monologue, or the testimony of a Bible character.

Types of Dramatizations

Drama in Christian education can vary from the simple and spontaneous to the elaborate and formal, depending on the teacher's objectives and goals. Remember that in using drama in education we are not concerned primarily with elaborate props, sets, and costumes. We are concerned with learning, with helping students experience and embody the truths of God's Word. Many types of drama can be adapted for all ages, while some are suited especially for children. Literally dozens of types of dramatizations are possible. This section will list many examples of dramatizations, and describe briefly a few of these.

Types of Drama for Children

Finger Play
Action Rhymes
Play-the-Story
Rhythm Games (may be used for Scripture memory)
Action Songs and Choruses

Finger Play: Children move their fingers to dramatize a rhyme, Bible verse, or story. Teachers can make up their own finger plays, or the class can make suggestions about words and actions they would like to include. Many Christian publishers have books of finger plays on a variety of subjects.

Play-the-Story: Children imagine what it would have been like to be in the situation of a Bible character. For example, they could act out some of the things David might have done while looking after his sheep. And others might even act out the sheep.

Types of Drama for All Ages

Story Telling
Object Lesson
Interview
Dialogue
Choral Reading
Litany
Conversational Scripture
Charades
Skit
Role Play
Faith Walk
Faith Circle
Pantomime, Mime Drama
Creative Movement
Tableaux, Living Picture
Monologue
Readers Theatre, Play Reading
Dramatic Reading
This is Your Life
T.V. Show
Puppetry
Shadow Play
Full-Length Drama
Musical Drama
8 mm Movie
Slide Presentation
Videotape Drama

Interview: The teacher or a class member assumes the role of a Bible character while another person assumes the role of a reporter doing a story on some incident in the Bible character's life.

Choral Reading: The teacher or class chooses a Bible passage, poem, song, prayer, or creative writing by one of the class members. The class may be divided into groups and soloists, or divided between men and women. The passage is then read dramatically, sometimes in unison, and sometimes in parts, or solos. If a Bible passage is used, it is necessary that every participant use the same translation. A copy may be provided by the teacher.

Role Play: A role play is spontaneous; no script is provided. The teacher outlines a biblical or present-day situation for the class, and chooses class members who will spontaneously act out the roles. When the role play has moved to its climax, the teacher stops the action and encourages class members to discuss what they have observed. Role players are encouraged to discuss their feelings and actions. Alternate ways of resolving the situation and biblical principles which apply to the situation may be discussed.

Faith Walk: The teacher allows himself to be blindfolded and asks one of the class members to lead him around the room. The guide is careful not to let the teacher bump into anything, verbally explaining where they are going, and any obstacles which need to be avoided. Class members are then divided into twos and take turns leading and being led. After the faith walk, the participants are encouraged to share their feelings, and discuss biblical principles of faith which they have experienced or observed.

Faith Circle: The teacher asks six students to sit and form a tight circle around him, their feet together around his feet as he stands in the center. Their arms should be extended up towards him. The teacher explains that he is going to fall backward and allow the class members to support him, so he will not fall to the floor. The teacher closes his eyes and turns around several times so he does not know the direction he is facing and falls while the students support him and pass him around the circle. Class members are encouraged to try this exercise in faith, and then discuss their feelings and the implications for their Christian life.

Pantomime: Because no speaking is involved with the movement, pantomime is a form of drama which is sometimes less threatening for those who have little experience with drama. Actors may silently act out a Bible or life situation, or a narrator may read while the actors pantomime.

Monologue: The teacher or class member assumes the character of a biblical, historical, or contemporary figure and tells his story. This may be especially effective in teaching a lesson relating to one biblical character or a missionary.

Readers Theater, Play Reading: A class may benefit from a good play without all the work of memorization and production. Characters are assigned, and members read the play.

Puppetry: Teachers or students manipulate puppets to illustrate a biblical, historical, or contemporary story or theme. Scripts, either purchased or written by teachers or class members, may be used, or puppets may speak spontaneously. A table, piano, or room divider may serve as a stage, or a puppet stage may be built. Puppets may be made from paper bags, socks, or purchased patterns. Commercial puppets are available in a variety of prices and qualities. Prerecorded tapes of puppet plays are commercially available, or may be produced by the teacher or class. your local Christian bookstore may carry scripts, patterns, and supplies.

Slide Presentation: The teacher and class decide together on a theme and objective. They assign responsibility for scenes, costumes, picture-taking and developing, narration, and assembling the final presentation. The slide presentation may be shown to the class or to the entire congregation.

Conclusion

We have seen that dramatization is frequently used in the Bible. We have noted the profound influence that drama can have on students' learning. But in order to use drama purposefully we must understand when, how, and with which groups to use it. All of this takes practice, but your efforts in dramatizing the lessons and in making Scripture personal will be richly rewarded by the enhanced learning of your students as they put God's Word into practice in their lives.

Dr. Ted Faszer holds an EdD in Adult and Higher Education and is currently assistant professor of Christian education and church music at North American Baptist Seminary in Sioux Falls, South Dakota. His wife, Marietta, has an MA in Elementary Education and teaches remedial reading at a public school.

Review Questions

1. If you meet a teacher who feels that drama has no place in Christian education, how could you explain the biblical and educational values of dramatic activities to this person?
2. Name several action-filled Bible stories which would lend themselves to some form of dramatization a) for children, b) for youth, c) for adults.
3. Why do you think many teachers lack confidence in using dramatic activities in their Bible teaching? How can these obstacles be overcome?

Application Activities

1. Look at your next unit of Sunday school lessons. Find and list the Bible verses, Bible stories, or real-life situations that could be taught by using dramatization. Plan to use one or more of these during the unit.
2. Prepare to lead your class in developing a simple biblical role play. Choose an appropriate Bible story for *your* age group you teach. Jot down information about the characters: ages, attitudes, actions, problems they face, and their relationships with God and with one another.

make posters as a Bible learning activity. Many inspiring and thought-provoking posters are available in Christian bookstores. A poster should be removed or replaced when it no longer attracts students' attention or conveys a message.

Puppets bring stories to life! Animation of many Bible events and modern life situations can be presented in class by using puppets. Simple finger puppets or those made with paper bags or socks can be used as effectively as the larger, full-body type. Time must be given to preparing the script and practicing with the puppet before using it in class. Puppets, scripts, and programs also are available for purchase through Christian bookstores.

Projected Visuals

Films add a dimension of realism and drama that cannot be achieved with other media. The impact of a well-chosen film will be seen in how the viewers respond to its message. Films also provide an excellent springboard for discussion to further the application of the message.

Filmstrips can be utilized for an introduction to a study or as a review. Instead of using an entire filmstrip, segments may be used to illustrate a point.

Both films and filmstrips should be introduced, pointing out their relation to the class session and how the information they present will be used. After viewing a film or filmstrip, use a quiz or discussion questions. Make the presentation of films or filmstrips an activity that leads to learning!

Transparencies are available for use with an overhead projector. Christian bookstores have access to professionally-produced transparencies of Bible maps, for teacher training, Bible survey, and other biblical studies. Some producers of materials provide only masters for making overhead transparencies. These masters can be easily made into attractive transparencies with the use of a heat-sensitive copier. Transparencies also can be handmade using colored transparency pens and clear acetate sheets.

Most churches have an overhead projector. It can be used in any room, with any lighting condition, with almost any age group.

Slides can be readily used for Bible teaching. Prepared sets of slides are available for illustrating lessons on a number of topics such as the life of Christ, the tabernacle, or other Bible stories. Often a tape also is provided with the narration for the slide presentation. Slides prepared by class members or a teacher provide great flexibility of use at a low cost.

Videocassettes use the medium of television. In Christian education the use of video resources is growing. Since the cost of equipment is decreasing, it is becoming more within the financial reach of many churches.

What the final form of video presentations will be is uncertain. However organizations that supply taped programs often are able to recommend and supply the right equipment for them.

A video recorder and camera can be used for videotaping church services and events. A teacher can do a self-evaluation by having a class session videotaped and then viewing it later.

Audio Aids

Records are available with a wide variety of music and stories for use in teaching situations. A number of children's musicals with a scriptural theme make enjoyable listening as well as teach biblical principles. Children can be taught an appreciation for Christian music. This might begin in the cradle roll department where music can be used to convey the peaceful atmosphere of God's house.

Tapes, especially cassettes, are a convenient, easy-to-use means of recording and playing back sound. There are numerous uses for tapes in a teaching situation. Recordings such as sermons, special lectures, or open-ended stories can be used to supplement lesson presentation and initiate discussion.

Practical Suggestions

In order to make the best use of audiovisual materials you should:

Preview

Preview the audiovisual aid you are planning to use. It is important to know the content of the aid and the way that it will be introduced and used in the class.

Prepare

Prepare ahead of time. Scheduling and reserving equipment far enough in advance will assure you of its availability. In addition, you should gather other items needed for the presentation, like extension cords and screen. You will find it more convenient if you set up *before* the class arrives.

Practice

Practice using the equipment and become familiar with it before using it in class. You should learn where all the controls are and how to operate them as well as make sure the equipment works properly.

Preserve

Preserve the effectiveness of an audiovisual. Using only one tool can also become dull. Student interest will decrease if they see the same medium in use all the time. It is better to use several methods and interchange them.

A good teacher will not make every class a media extravaganza. Simple, well-presented lessons can be more effective than ones that require the use of much electronic equipment.

Conclusion

You, as a Christian teacher, have an important mission in communicating the life-changing Word of God. Every available means should be used to ensure that the message is received and understood by those whose lives are being shaped by it.

Student interest is vital and using varied channels of communication will draw students into the class session. Audiovisuals are your tools to communicate the Word in a variety of ways and knowing how to use these tools inproves the levels of communication and learning. Student interest is greater when each student is actively involved in the learning process. The goal is application of Bible truths in the lives of the students.

For effective communication you must rely on the Lord, the designer and master of communication. He will enable you

to reach and teach your students more effectively as you sincerely utilize the various methods available to you.

Dennis Bouchard is a Christian education consultant who specializes in the use of audiovisuals. He was formerly on the staff of Washington Bible College, Lanham, Maryland.

Review Questions

1. What are some obstacles in communication?
2. What are the channels of communication created by God in man?
3. Why did God use visual aids?
4. Explain how the teacher can get students actively involved in the learning process.
5. Why is it important for Christian teachers to get students interested and involved?
6. List three different uses for each of the following audiovisuals: a) bulletin board, b) chart, c) graph, d) learning center, e) model.

7. What is the purpose of introducing films, filmstrips, or cassettes?
8. What are the advantages of the overhead projector?
9. Explain the four "Practical Suggestions" for use of audiovisuals.

Application Activities

1. Using a lesson plan, such as the one in a Sunday school teacher's manual, list as many different audiovisual tools that *could* be used in teaching that lesson. Choose one or two tools that would be the most effective and plan how to include them in teaching that lesson.
2. Practice writing on a chalkboard. Emphasize the important words by circling, underlining, or writing them with colored chalk.
3. Prepare an overhead transparency to be used in teaching a class. Taking an idea from a teacher's manual or Scripture passage, create a visual to illustrate that idea.
4. Begin a personal picture file by setting up general categories and filing pictures gathered from magazines and curriculum resource packets.
5. If your church has movie and/or filmstrip projectors, learn how to load and run each.

objectively see yourself the way you are. In the seminary classroom where I teach a course called "Teaching Practicum," I've discovered over and over again that as the students are evaluated after their teaching experience, they are utterly shocked to hear from the class what they have said and what they have done.

You do not have the capability of objectively observing yourself. That's one of the reasons why you need other friends in the church. The body of Christ can become an effective tool of helping you improve your teaching ministry. You are able to gloss over your weaknesses. Others are needed to help you get the job of evaluation done. But ultimately, you have to honestly see yourself and how you function.

Second, it is difficult to evaluate your own teaching because everyone has a "defense mechanism." That mechanism is always lurking around a corner, waiting to strike out at anyone who dares to step on your performance. That mechanism is quick to come to your aid when you are threatened.

Because of this, you will have to work extra hard to alleviate that defense mechanism and work diligently to open your eyes to see who you are and how you're functioning.

One type of evaluation program requires that someone record everything observed during an hour of teaching. Then you evaluate your effectiveness by contrasting your performance with your standard.

Get an outsider to help you see how you are functioning. If a standard has been established, even a good friend whom you respect and trust can help you do the evaluation. A Sunday school superintendent, director of Christian education, professor of Christian education, or an educational consultant might also provide this service.

Evaluate the product as well as the process of teaching—The most meaningful way to evaluate your teaching is to see what is happening to the students. If they are changing and growing in Christ as a result of your classes, you are effectively communicating the Word of God to them. If you see only minor or superficial changes taking place, you need to take a closer look at how you are relating to them and the methods you are using.

Rating Yourself as a Teacher

As was explained earlier, you will want to ask yourself some questions about your own teaching to start your evaluation process.

Design an evaluation form—To get started with your evaluation, you might want to design a rating form. On the last page of this leaflet you will find a sample form that may be used to evaluate your teaching.

It is difficult to provide one form that will be applicable to all grade levels and situations. The one provided here is an attempt to design one that will be relevant to all situations and, because it is all-encompassing, it tends to be weaker than one you might design.

If you make up your own form, you will want to keep the needs and interests of your own particular age group in mind in writing the statements.

Involve the entire school—Your entire school ought to be regularly involved in evaluation. These evaluations should include the administrative process of your school, the people-involvement of the staff, the use of space and equipment, and the grouping or grading of the students. There is virtually no end to the evaluation which can be conducted. The purpose of this article is to help you see the possibilities and to get you started.

Treat individual problems separately—As you are grading yourself, if only a few students

in your class would cause you to record a low performance grade, you may want to zero in on those few and find out what their particular problems or needs are and work on solving them. Remember, all students are different, each has individual needs and desires. If there are just one or two problem students in your class, the need for change may be theirs and not yours.

Seek ways your teaching may be enriched—In evaluating over 3000 teachers in American churches, I found that people don't mind being evaluated as long as a meaningful way of improving their ministry is provided as a result. In fact, they are generally very open to it.

Once you have identified your weaknesses, various resources

Evaluation can cause growth in your own spiritual life and in the lives of your students, and bring numerical growth to your church.

may be consulted to help you find ways to make improvements. Resources may be found in complete teacher training courses, Christian education texts, how-to manuals, and from various resource persons in your community.

Repeat the evaluation process periodically—Once an initial evaluation has taken place, the process is not complete. Evaluation must continue. Pinpointing a weak area and attempting to strengthen it doesn't necessarily mean you have succeeded in improving in that area. After a period of time you need to go through the process again to see if the same weaknesses still appear.

Above all, don't be afraid of evaluation. It is an effective tool for improving your teaching ministry. When used consistently and continually it can cause growth in your own spiritual life and in the lives of your students, and bring numerical growth to your church.

Harold J. Westing is assistant professor of Christian education at Conservative Baptist Theological Seminary in Denver, Colorado. Previously he was director of Christian education for the Conservative Baptist Association of America. For many years he served as a consultant to local churches and state and regional associations conducting evaluations of Christian education programs.

Review Questions

1. In what ways can *informal* evaluations affect your class?
2. Name the three goals of any teaching ministry and explain why it is vital to include all of them.
3. Why is self-evaluation difficult?
4. Once an area of weakness is discovered in your teaching, what should be your next step?
5. In what practical and specific ways can you evaluate the "products" of your teaching?
6. Describe the characteristics of a good evaluation form.
7. Why is evaluation a continual process?

An Evaluation of Christian Teaching

Grade yourself on each of the five areas in this evaluation form. The five statements with their subpoints provide a comprehensive definition of what an effective teacher does in the teaching process. Be objective and honest as you rate yourself for each statement. Do not attempt to tally your ratings or compare them with another teacher's score. Rate yourself to see where your strengths are and what areas need improvement.

Read each statement and circle one of the letters which precede it. Circle "A" for always; "O" for often; "S" for seldom; and "N" for never.

TRAINING WHEN MEETING

I. Motivating Students to Grow

A O S N 1. I study each student's needs and design lessons to meet those needs.
A O S N 2. I present lessons that inspire students to apply scriptural truths to their lives.
A O S N 3. I introduce lessons in such a way that students want to continue to study.
A O S N 4. I develop an atmosphere which encourages students to freely express their beliefs and doubts.
A O S N 5. I encourage students to discover the truths of the Word of God for themselves.
A O S N 6. I use activities which involve students in the learning process.
A O S N 7. I use a variety of teaching methods.
A O S N 8. I present interesting and life-related illustrations which draw the student into the lesson.
A O S N 9. I treat individual student's learning difficulties with sensitivity.

II. Designing and Directing the Teaching-Learning Process to Implement Spiritual Growth

A O S N 1. I observe behavioral changes in my students.
A O S N 2. I adapt lesson truths so that they apply to the students' age level.
A O S N 3. I focus the truths of God's Word to meet individual student's needs.
A O S N 4. I motivate students' feelings so they are stirred to act upon the truth taught.

III. Building Disciplinary Relationships

A O S N 1. I show a personal interest in each student and am able to interact with each one about who they are.
A O S N 2. I contact students who are absent.
A O S N 3. I plan class social and fellowship activities.
A O S N 4. I follow up life-related learning activities which were assigned in class.
A O S N 5. I pray regularly for students' needs.
A O S N 6. I visit students in their homes to better understand their life situations.
A O S N 7. I encourage students to work toward self-discipline.
A O S N 8. I guide students to experience salvation in Jesus Christ.

IV. Structuring an Effective Learning Environment

A O S N 1. I coordinate classroom decorations with each quarter's lesson aims.
A O S N 2. I make sure chairs and tables are the proper size for the students.
A O S N 3. I use a variety of audiovisual aids in the teaching process.
A O S N 4. I promote a sense of well-being and enthusiasm for learning.

V. Participating as a Team Member

A O S N 1. I plan objectives with other members of the department on a regular basis.
A O S N 2. I follow the assigned curriculum plan established for the class.
A O S N 3. I participate in departmental activities.
A O S N 4. I follow my supervisor's guidance.
A O S N 5. I attend seminars or special training courses to improve and enrich my teaching skills.